STEPHEN CURRY

RISE OF THE STAR

JOHN EMERSON

Stephen Curry: Rise of the Star

Copyright © 2016 by John Emerson.

CONTENTS

INTRODUCTION

'I've never been afraid of big moments. I get butterflies. I get nervous and anxious, but I think those are all good signs that I'm ready for the moment' – Stephen Curry

12 MINUTES. 12 MORE MINUTES was all it took for Stephen Curry and his Warriors to finally bring home the coveted Larry O'Brien Trophy, and be forever immortalized as champions. It was the 4th Quarter in Game 6 of the 2015 NBA Finals, with the Golden State Warriors playing in the Cleveland Cavaliers' home ground. Going into the 4th quarter, they held the lead and were just 1 more quarter away from winning an NBA championship. However, just 3 games ago, the whole world was counting the Warriors out.

Being initially down 2-1 in the series against LeBron James' Cleveland Cavaliers, many fans started to entertain the thought that the Cavs (even without their 2 superstars in Kyrie Irving and Kevin Love) would steal the championship away from the Warriors. After all, many people thought that they didn't even deserve to be in the NBA finals in the first place.

All the skeptics begin to surface once more, as did the talk of the Golden State Warriors being 'lucky' to have reached this far into the NBA Playoffs in the first place. They were 'lucky' that the Oklahoma City Thunder lost its MVP in Kevin Durant due to injury.

They were 'lucky' that they weren't contending with the previous champions, the San Antonio Spurs. They were 'lucky' to be even contending for an NBA Title at all.

These skeptics and haters were all too familiar to Curry. Throughout his entire basketball journey (as you will learn throughout this book), he has faced countless criticisms and doubts, only to overcome them all and emerge triumphant despite adversity. He was determined to do it again now in the biggest stage of basketball.

Stephen Curry was intent in showing the world that he was not just 'lucky' – he wanted to show that he *deserved* to be playing in the Finals. He *deserved* to be the MVP. He *deserved* to win a championship. He *deserved* to be recognised as one of the greatest players to ever play this game.

From humble beginnings, as the 7th pick in the 2009 NBA Draft that went relatively unnoticed, from having the one of worst records in the NBA in his first year as a Warrior, from being cast aside by critics for being always riddled with injury, he was now on the verge of ending all speculation once and for all as to whether his name deserved to be mentioned amongst the NBA greats.

All it took was just 12 more minutes, just 1 more quarter of basketball – with the Cleveland Cavalier fans booing him, the critics doubting him and the whole world watching him - he would show them just what he's capable of to succeed under pressure, a skill he had picked up and honed over all the years of his basketball life. After 12 minutes, the world would come to know of the legend of Stephen Curry – being one of the greatest shooters to ever play the game of basketball. After 12 more minutes, Stephen Curry would be deemed a bonafide superstar. After 12 more minutes, Stephen Curry wouldn't be known as the guy who got 'lucky' to be MVP – he would go from being just another all-star, to being an NBA Champion and solidifying his status as an absolute force to be reckoned with in the league.

This story is about the rise of Stephen Curry, the Long-Shot, the MVP, and the Champion.

CHAPTER 1

EARLY CHILDHOOD

'Be the best version of yourself in anything that you do. You don't have to live anybody else's story' – Stephen Curry

FROM AN EARLY AGE, Wardell Stephen Curry was gifted with a talent for basketball. Being born into a family with not only a tremendous liking for the sport, but also a history of professional playing time, he was exposed to the game at a very young age.

His father was Dell Curry, a former professional NBA player, and he played for teams such as the Utah Jazz, Cleveland Cavaliers, Charlotte Hornets, Milwaukee Bucks and Toronto Raptors.

Needless to say, the love of basketball was instilled in him at a ripe and tender age. Dell would often bring his sons, Steph and his brother Seth, to his games where they would join his father for warm-ups. By watching and practicing with his father, he would learn and pick up the fundamentals of the game of basketball. When his father went on road trips with his team, his mother would step in to fill the coaching – training him and instilling discipline and hard work into his daily routine. From a young age, he had already had a feel for stepping onto an NBA court and tasted the rigors of hard work that came with being an NBA player. Who knew that these early experiences would shape a young boy with a love for the game into a future MVP and NBA champion.

Steph was no stranger to winning basketball games – and winning a lot of them. As this book is being written, the Warriors have the best record in the entire league for the 2015 – 2016 NBA season, and are possibly en route to having the best win-loss record we've seen from an NBA team ever since Michael Jordan's Chicago Bulls era.

Even early on in his basketball career, he had a knack for winning games. From 2001 to 2002 while his father was playing for the Toronto Raptors, Stephen attended Queensway Christian College in Toronto, Ontario. As a player on his basketball team, he would finally get a taste of what it was like to be an undisputed winner, as he led his grades 7 and 8 basketball team to an undefeated season.

While Curry was making a name for himself as a local prodigy in his small town and school, his father also had his fair share of achievements. As a member of the Charlotte Hornets for 10 seasons, he earned the Sixth Man of The Year Award and currently still ranks as one of the all-time leaders in points, games played, and 3-point field goal percentage for the franchise. As a college player, Dell Curry was also in Virginia Tech's Hall of Fame.

Stephen was not oblivious to the growing reputation of Curry's father as an NBA player. His father played a pivotal part as a role model for Steph, as he grew up and as his game developed over the years. He would work tirelessly to ensure that one day he would eclipse the status of his mentor.

He was determined to not be known as just Dell Curry's son. He wanted to carve out his own legacy, and live a story of his own.

CHAPTER 2

HIGH SCHOOL BASKETBALL

'We have to have the mentality that we have to work for everything we're going to get' – Stephen Curry

HIGH SCHOOL WAS THE PERFECT PLATFORM for Stephen to finally showcase his years of hard work on the hardwood floor. Wanting to show the world exactly what years of hard work had done for his game, he would finally get a glimpse of what real-life competitive basketball would feel like.

While the undefeated seasons at his Queensway Christian College were great learning experiences for him, they were child's play in Curry's eyes and they went relatively unnoticed by everyone else. High school basketball is the first stage for any up-and-coming basketball superstar to start making a name and reputation for himself, as college scouts would recruit the high school players which seemed to have a lot of potential.

Steph was going to get a taste of the limelight for the first time and he was finally ready to taste a higher level of competition. With his experience of the NBA player's work ethic, this future star would shine the brightest amongst all the other players.

* * *

The Birth of a Shooter

However, things weren't always easy for Steph in high school. Doubts begin to follow Steph whenever scouts or fans watched him play. Everywhere he went, coaches and critics would say the same thing: "He is just too small."

Being only a mere five-foot-three Guard with a skinny frame, he would struggle when matching up against bigger and more experienced players. Even though he could definitely shoot the ball (a skill he picked up from his father), he had to shoot it from his waist, and not from above his head like a normal player would.

In his mind, Steph had already made the decision to do whatever it took to get him a basketball scholarship to one of the premier basketball colleges in the nation. But to do so, there was no way he could make it with his scrawny frame and novice shooting form.

So Steph and his father worked tirelessly, day and night, to improve his shooting form and finally master the art of the jump shot. These training sessions were brutally tiring, and mentally taxing for the young high school kid. His father would break down his shot into a series of distinct and subtle movements – and he broke it down so much that at some points Steph could not even shoot the ball anymore – feeling completely stuck. He felt completely stifled when having to work through each motion, and was so adamant in making sure that he perfected it that sometimes when he fell short of perfection, he would cry on the court due to sheer frustration. It was a painful time for Steph, but these growing pains were pivotal in producing one of the greatest shooters to ever grace an NBA court.

All that hard work paid off over the summer, and now with a couple of inches added to his height, he was an undoubtedly much improved basketball player.

Steph would go on to be named all-state and all-conference, while leading his team to 3 conference titles and 3 state playoff appearances.

Those accolades made Steph proud of his achievements, but he knew that ultimately, they only served one purpose – to get him a college basketball scholarship.

As his father enrolled in Virginia Tech as a college player (and made a legendary status for himself as one of their best players), naturally Steph wanted to follow in his footsteps. However, Virginia Tech had other plans for Steph. The same concerns and comments arose once again – he was simply too small of a player and not athletic enough. Because of this, no elite basketball school thought he was good enough to play college ball and make an impact. These early rejections ignited a burning drive in Steph, to the point where his relentless work ethic would cause him to make one of the biggest impacts in the game of basketball today.

Virginia Tech only offered Steph a chance to join the team as a walk-on player, an offer which Curry felt devastated by. He knew he was going to be overshadowed by his father's legacy there and probably would not get the playing time he deserved, so he refused their offer and looked at the options that *were* given to him. He knew that he had much more potential than the world believed he had, and even when everyone was counting him out, he kept his head high and believed in himself.

However, his choices looked bleak.

Three colleges offered him scholarships: Davidson College, Virginia Commonwealth University (VCU) and Winthrop University.

These schools did not have top-tier basketball teams, but they were all Stephen had to work with. Steph doubted as to whether he would ever make it to the NBA at all or would he go unnoticed in one of these low-key schools. Yet, despite having everything against him, he decided to turn this weakness into a strength.

Stephen chose to attend Davidson College, whose basketball team had not won an NCAA tournament game since 1969. Stephen figured if nobody was paying attention to this no-name school that had had no winning basketball culture in ages, he was going to *force* them to pay attention.

Little did we know, this six-foot point guard would go on to make history as one of the greatest Davidson basketball players to ever step onto their court.

CHAPTER 3

COLLEGE BASKETBALL

'If you don't fall how are you going to know what getting up is like?' – Stephen Curry

FOR THE FIRST TIME in Stephen Curry's life, he knew what it felt like to have his dreams take a detour. Here was a young man who had his life planned out for him. A professional basketball player as a father, having undefeated seasons in middle school, an illustrious career in high school and yet, he had fallen – his goal of attending Virginia Tech, or one of the other elite basketball colleges had been denied to him.

But there was one thing the world could not take away from him – his drive and work ethic. He knew he had a slim chance of making the world pay attention, and after his dream fell flat on its face, he had only one goal – to get back up and put Davidson back on college basketball's map.

As a freshman, the basketball court was a stage and Curry was the main star of the show. He led the Southern Conference in scoring with 21.5 points per game. In the entire nation, he finished second in scoring behind another future NBA star, Kevin Durant. He broke the freshman scoring record for his school while playing against Chattanooga. He was named the Southern Conference Freshman Player of The Year, the Southern Conference Tournament MVP while being selected to the Southern Conference All-Tournament Team, All Freshman Team and first team All-SoCon. After the season had ended, he was selected by Team USA to appear at the 2007 FIBA Under-19 World Championships, where he won a Silver Medal.

Stephen was gathering accolade after accolade, and his achievements were piling up one after another. However, one goal still seemed to elude him – he was unable to lead Davidson to their first NCAA tournament win in over three decades. Not wavering in his commitment, these early experiences as a freshman were vital for him to hone his skills and to get a feel for college basketball – experiences he would need if he wanted to achieve his ultimate goal.

He had faced setbacks before, and this one was no different. He had set out to make a name for himself while raising Davidson's status to an elite basketball team – and he was going to do just that. Not deterred by his NCAA loss to University of Maryland in his freshman season, he went back to work, making sure that his sophomore season would be much different.

With an extra three inches added to his frame, the now six-foot-three Stephen Curry added a whole new dimension to his game. Once again, he led the Southern Conference in scoring and helped Davidson earn its thirth straight NCAA Tournament bid in his sophomore year. Steph had all the tools, experience and resources needed to achieve the recognition he so greatly desired. After qualifying for the NCAA tournament, it was time for him to finally make history.

* * *

Breakthrough

March 21st, 2008. After not winning an NCAA tournament for close to 40 years now, the Davidson basketball team was more than ready to end their dry spell. They knew they had what it took to finally break through and put their names in basketball relevance once again. They were tried and tested for glory just a season ago, but came up short in a disappointing loss. With a season to ponder over their loss, and the blood, sweat and tears that came with wanting another opportunity to win, their chance had finally come.

Davidson was up against Gonzaga University.

Right from the opening tip-off, Gonzaga took an early 5 point lead against Davidson. Davidson's offense seemed scattered and disorganized – maybe due to the nerves that they felt from playing such an important game. In the next play however, Steph quickly rolled off a screen, fumbled his hands a little before hoisting up a mid-range jump shot. Davidson finally scored their first 2 points after 2 excruciatingly long minutes – calming down the team and their home crowd fans.

This was the usual theme throughout the first half of the game, with Davidson trying their very best to keep up with Gonzaga's punches. Curry was pulling out all stops, doing all that he could to keep his team alive and contending. But despite his efforts in the beginning, Davidson still found themselves losing to Gonzaga.

Deflated and tired out, Davidson was trailing Gonzaga by 5 points at the half. Once the second half started, they found the lead swiftly increasing to 11 points, and the nerves that were so evident in the first half of the game seemed to get the better of Davidson.

This situation was all too familiar to Curry – after all, it was only last year when they faced the pain of a similar loss to another team. Throughout his entire life, he was constantly faced with people saying that he wasn't good enough, constantly looking down on him and belittling his potential – and every single time, he has proved them wrong. This time would be no different.

He was not going to let the same mistake happen twice. If he was to make a name for himself, there would be no bigger stage than right there at that very moment. He had a choice, to either let Davidson succumb to its all too familiar state of losing NCAA games, or finally break through, and make basketball history.

Steph chose to make history.

He went on an absolute scoring tear, hitting 8 for 10 three pointers from the field, and scoring 30 points in the second half alone. Curry finished with 40 points, exhausted, burned out, but most importantly – victorious.

Stunning the Gonzaga team and audiences watching around the world, he single-handedly willed his team to victory over Gonzaga and led his team to their first NCAA victory since 1969. Everyone finally started to pay full attention to Davidson and what was in store for them. Once again, he faced adversity and emerged triumphant.

However, their breakthrough did not stop there. After finally conquering their past and breaking their dry spell of losing, it was time to defeat other teams, and conquer the college basketball landscape.

Once again, Curry and his team were faced with massive doubters as they entered their second game – this time against the heavy favorite, Georgetown University. Georgetown was famous for its storied and rich basketball culture throughout history. Everyone knows that great NBA legends are made in Georgetown, with legends like Patrick Ewing and Allen Iverson enrolling in it.

Needless to say, everyone was expecting a walk-over by Georgetown over the small up-and-coming

Davidson – and for the first half, their predictions were right. The situation could not have looked bleaker for Davidson, being down 17 points at the half with Curry only scoring 5 points. But once again, Curry refused to let anybody get in the way of his dreams. While everyone was counting Davidson out, Curry had to step up and let them know exactly what his team was made of. After all, the stage had just gotten bigger now that Davidson had just won their first game, and Curry was more than prepared to put on another amazing show.

With only one half left to spare to win the game against Georgetown, Curry went on another scoring rampage, pouring in 25 points in the second half alone, willing his team to an amazing comeback victory by only 4 points and shocking the world in the process once again. David had just beaten Goliath, and if people weren't believers in Davidson before, they sure were then. If they still refused to pay attention to Steph after their first win, people now had no choice but to watch and marvel at a rising star making history right in front of their very eyes - proving each and every one of his doubters wrong. Davidson had officially gone from zero to hero in a couple of years since Stephen Curry arrived.

Their new found reign of terror on other basketball teams would still not end, as they picked up yet another win against the third-seeded Wisconsin. The flair for dramatic comebacks had quieted down during this game, as the Davidson Wildcats were in control of the game and finished Wisconsin off in definitive style. Curry finished the game with 33 points, making him 1 of only 4 college players to ever score 30 or more points in their first four career NCAA tournament games.

Davidson's new found glory would tragically end before reaching the promise land and bringing home the championship. In a match against the top-seeded Kansas Jayhawks, they faced an excruciating painful loss by only 2 points, and Kansas went on to win the championship that season.

In Steph's historic run to college stardom, he beat the official college 3-point record for a single season, eclipsing the record of 158.

Davidson was devastated, for having gone so far only be halted in his tracks. However, Stephen's second season proved valuable to him, as not only did he make Davidson history by finally winning NCAA tournament games and even bringing Davidson to the Elite 8, he had solidified his status as a force to be reckoned with in the college basketball scene - getting the recognition he deserved. The NBA had now turned its head and had its eyes wide open, watching and waiting for when Curry was about to make the big leap and officially bring his exciting brand of basketball to the grandest stage of all.

However, the NBA dream had to wait. Being loyal to Davidson, Steph announced that he was going to return for his junior year for one more shot at bringing a historic run to Davidson, and trying to heal the old wounds that he had suffered when losing to Kansas. He also wanted to develop his game further as a point guard, knowing full well that that would be his future playing position in the NBA.

Curry's junior year showcased his peak performance as a collegiate athlete. All the hard work and years of practice from his early childhood and his first few years in college were clearly paying off now, as he set career highs in point in a game, 44, as well as passing the 2000 point mark for his career and setting the record for most points scored for his school. His junior season proved to be one of many ups and downs for Stephen, losing narrowly to other teams such as Oklahoma, facing ankle injuries against Furman and even going scoreless against Loyola. Disappointingly, the Wildcats failed to get an NCAA tournament bid. In Curry's final game as a Wildcat, he scored 26 points, and had 9 rebounds and 5 assists in a game for the 2009 National Invitation Tournament. He finished off his college career as the NCAA scoring leader and was named a consensus first team All-American.

Steph had given all he could to Davidson, and by the end of the season, he knew he had to move on. This time, Steph knew exactly which goal to pursue next, as he turned around to meet the NBA's eyes that were already looking at him - awaiting his arrival from afar.

CHAPTER 4

NBA CAREER

'Basketball was mine, and that's what carried me to this point' – Stephen Curry

DAVID STERN, the NBA Commissioner emerged from backstage, and walked slowly to the podium with a slight grin on his face. After taking a breath, he looked at the crowd and began, *'With the 7th pick in the 2009 NBA Draft, the Golden State Warriors select, Stephen Curry from Davidson College.'*

It was the 2009 NBA Draft, and Stephen Curry had with him his family as they waited patiently for him to finally make his leap into the big leagues. After David Stern made his announcement, Steph was rewarded with loud cheers and congratulations from his family and friends for making it this far into his basketball career. A little kid who had a dream, had finally achieved the biggest one of all – making it to the pros.

Crowds of people cheered, crowds of people booed, while some were quiet. The boos came from a large portion of the New York Knicks' fans, who wanted the Knicks to select Curry instead of the

Warriors. A lot of people knew that the kid coming out from Davidson College was going to be special, after his historic legacy in college.

Yet, he would still face doubters wherever he went. Even at the highest level, he faced the same criticisms – being too small, too scrawny, too weak and not athletic enough. He had probably gotten used to these comments by now, and the NBA was the best place to dispel those comments once and for all.

While some teams and fans desperately wanted Steph to join and bring glory to their teams, the pressure was definitely on now for Steph to perform up to the highest standards of basketball. After all, the NBA isn't like college, as evidenced by many college superstars who faded into obscurity once they joined the NBA. The NBA was an entirely different league, different game and had its own set of rules. It would either make, or break you as a player. He was aware of this due to his father's past experience as an NBA player, and was up for the challenge. All his life he had fought through battles and obstacles, and now finally his time had come.

To the average NBA watcher, Stephen Curry's rise

to prominence might have seemed completely sudden or unannounced. Everybody knows who Stephen Curry is right now, being an MVP, an NBA champion and one of the greatest shooters to ever play this game – but not everybody knows the rollercoaster ride that Curry had to endure before finally rising to fame.

* * *

Growing Pains

Right from the start, Steph came in to the league with determination to prove his worth in the NBA.

Curry's first year in the league was pretty solid for a rookie. He finished 2nd in NBA Rookie Of The Year Voting and was named to the NBA All-Rookie First Team. Pretty good – but by no means an outstanding player. Nobody expected Curry to suddenly break out into one of the best players of our time. He was always under the radar, and other fellow rookies overshadowed him. For example, the first overall pick that year Blake Griffin, was making headlines all around the league for his explosive dunks and sky-high highlights. Everybody agreed, that in a couple of years Blake would be an elite player in the league. Yet, nobody gave that kind of attention to Steph. Once again, he was being cast aside, and forced to make a name for himself.

The journey to stardom wasn't as smooth as he'd liked. In his subsequent years in the league, he was riddled with injuries to his right ankle, which caused him to sit out most of the regular season games. This was intensely frustrating for Curry – being plagued with injury, and with his team holding a mediocre record, his future began to look bleak once again. But by no means was he going to fade into obscurity in the NBA just like all the other college players that came before him. He knew what he had to offer in his game, and he wanted to make sure everybody else knew as well.

**

The Splash Brothers

Players win games, but teams win championships.

If there was any way for Steph to be taken seriously, he could not do it by himself. Just as the greatest conquests throughout history are not the work of a single conqueror, but also of his loyal army, Steph knew he needed to have a good team for him to contend in the league, let alone make a splash. In just a couple of years, another key player would be added to the Warriors that would make Curry's name forever associated with that "splash".

Klay Thompson was selected as the 11th pick in the 2011 NBA draft. He was a versatile shooting guard, primarily known for his ability to shoot but not so much his athletic ability. Just like Curry before, he did not garner as much attention as all the previous players that were selected before him. Needless to say, Curry and Thompson were underdogs in the league, and this underdog mentality would fuel them to make a name for themselves as one of the best 3-point duos the league has ever witnessed.

The Splash Brothers were born.

In his 4th NBA season, Curry would finally begin to break out of his shell. The Warriors had just offered him a new 4 year contract, and many critics and analysts were doubting Curry could live up to it – being riddled with injuries all the time. This refocused Curry's drive, and after a year of sitting out games, going through the growing pains of being initiated to the NBA, and a solid team around him, he was now back and finally ready to make his mark in the league.

The next couple of years finally looked brighter for Curry and the Warriors. They were qualifying for the NBA playoffs, but often falling short in the second round. The Splash Brothers were a household favorite as more and more people would gather to watch the 3-point spectacle of Curry and Thompson in the backcourt, earning Curry multiple All-Star nominations. He even set the Golden State Warrior record for most career three-pointers, while only in his fifth season.

All around the league, fans, analysts and players started to take notice of the up and coming all-star. Everybody knew that Stephen was a great player, and it seemed like he was getting the attention he finally deserved. In just a couple more seasons, Curry and the Warriors would no longer just be referred to as 'good', but would go on to make history.

Curry's jersey number was 30, the same number

his father wore when he was an NBA player. All his life, his father-mentor was always someone to look up to, someone to admire, someone to beat. Stephen had followed in his father's footsteps, joined the NBA and was now one of the premier players the league had ever seen. As far as his father was concerned, Stephen had eclipsed him a long time ago. But Stephen was not satisfied with simply being another good player. All those years of practicing drills, instilling discipline and hard work into himself had taught him that he could achieve literally anything he set his mind to do – and this time, his mind was set on a much bigger, loftier goal – being the best player in the league.

* * *

Rise to MVP

Once again, the New York Knicks found themselves stunned, and once again, it was due to the Golden State Warriors. Only a couple of years ago in the NBA Draft the Knicks were vying to draft Stephen Curry, only for him to be stolen away by the Warriors. Now before the start of the 2014-2015 NBA season, history would repeat itself.

The President of the New York Knicks' basketball operations, Phil Jackson, had been wanting Steve Kerr to take over the Knicks' head coaching job and lead them under a new playing system. After all, Phil had coached Steve several years before, leading him and the Chicago Bulls to multiple championship runs. It was only normal that Steve would join forces with his previous coach and try to bring glory to a now rebuilding Knicks team. While everyone had expected Steve to grab the coaching job right away, Steve had other plans.

In May 2014, the Warriors announced that they had just hired Steve Kerr as their new head coach. The world was stunned, as the Warriors had once again stolen from right under the Knicks' noses. These few 'steals' in Steph and then Steve Kerr, would make all the difference in the Warriors going on to be one of the most dominant forces the league had ever encountered.

A new playing system was implemented, with the Warriors having a more fast-paced style of play and Curry having more freedom to do what he does best – shoot. Coupled with other key players being added to their team or having developed over the years, namely Draymond Greene, Harrison Barnes and Andre Iguodala, the Warriors were now a legitimate threat to the entire league and primed to raise Curry's star status to new heights.

As soon as the 2014-2015 NBA season started, Stephen Curry was now no longer just another good player. Just like in his earlier school years, he began collecting accolade after accolade. He was now the leading vote-getter for the 2015 All-Star team. He broke his own 3-point league record, and became the fastest player in NBA history to reach 1000 career 3-pointers. Stephen had always been a wild lion hungry to escape from its cage and showcase its reign of terror within the league – and now he had the perfect supporting cast around him to set him loose.

Under Steve Kerr's guidance and Curry's unprecedented shooting skills, the Warriors finished as the best team in the entire league, collecting a whopping 67 wins in the process. In just a couple of years, the same Stephen Curry who was facing injuries, doubters and critics had now emerged victorious once again - proving everybody wrong.

* * *

MVP

'I've got to start with my wife,' Steph choked on his words a bit.

There was a subtle pause, and everyone in the room could feel the emotions Steph was speaking with. In the seats in front of him there were a swarm of reporters, all waiting eagerly to hear what Steph had to say after receiving the NBA's Most Valuable Player Award. But all the media attention did not matter to him as much as his family did.

A couple of rows ahead was his entire support group – his wife, his parents, his brother, his little daughter and other family members all gathered to witness Curry achieve his dream.

Only a couple of weeks prior, it had been made official that Stephen Curry was now deemed the NBA's MVP. By leading his team to the best record in the NBA for that season, Steph's stardom had risen beyond anyone's expectation and the MVP trophy was the defining piece that made everything else worth it.

'Steph Curry. You're the leader of the team which has the best record in the NBA this season. This is a tribute, not just to you but the entire organization, and the great fans here in the Bay Area,' Adam Silver announced proudly, as the loud cheers of Warrior fans echoed throughout the entire stadium.

Fast forward a couple of days, and now Steph was on the Warriors home court with the new NBA Comissioner, Adam Silver standing next to him. Crowds of Warrior fans had waited ages for this glorious moment to happen, and now their time had finally arrived.

He continued 'So it's my honor, and my pleasure to present you Steph Curry, with the 2014-2015 Kia MVP Award!'

The Warrior fans exploded in excitement, and the cheers became so deafening that Steph could not even speak for a second. All Steph did was raise the MVP Trophy as high as he could, looking at the proud fans that he had amassed throughout his NBA career thus far. All those years of hard work, discipline and constantly battling the haters and obstacles – this had truly become the defining moment of his career. Only at the young age of 27, he had a long way to go in the NBA, and the MVP trophy signified a new beginning for Stephen Curry as a member of NBA elite.

He looked at his home fans with pride while still carrying the MVP Trophy. He knew, there was only one other thing to do to bring more joy to the Warrior franchise.

It was time to win a championship.

CHAPTER 5

CURRENT PERSONAL LIFE

'I try and use every game as an opportunity to witness...When I step on the floor people should know who I represent, who I believe in' – Stephen Curry

THE WARRIOR FANS were on their feet, relishing the show that Steph was putting on for them. He's in a completely different zone – draining a barrage of 3-pointers as his opponents and fans can do nothing but stare in awe. As Steph raises up for another 3-pointer, the announcer yells "Curry, for 3 once again..... GOOOD!!! He drains another 3!"

Steph smiles, pounds his chest and points

upwards towards the sky.

Warrior fans are acquainted with that very gesture. After all the years of playing, he never fails to remind himself of the cause of his success in the first place.

Whenever he makes an incredible shot, achieves something remarkable or before he even steps on the basketball court, he humbles himself by pounding his chest and pointing to the sky, a symbol of his dedication to his faith and religion. He knows he could not have gotten where he is today without the help of God.

Stephen has always been a family-oriented person. Following his father's footsteps and cementing his legacy in the game of basketball, he also credits his success to many of his other family members, as well as his faith towards his religion.

A couple rows back in the seats, familiar faces would frequent his games, and would cheer him on excessively – giving him the support and confidence he needs to perform the way he does.

His mother, Sonya Curry, would give a standing ovation for her son during the games. This was the same woman who instilled the sense of discipline in Steph, teaching him the meaning of hard work and constant practice even when his father wasn't around to coach him. Next to her would be Ayesha Curry, Steph's loyal and loving wife who has been with Steph ever since they were 14 years old. On Ayesha's lap, tiny Riley Curry would be taking in the amazing sights and sounds of the Oracle Arena (the Warriors' home court), confused as to what all the commotion is about. Little does she know just how much of a superstar her dad has become.

Game 5, 2015 NBA Finals – Curry's family was in the crowd once again, and the Warriors are now a couple of minutes away from clinching a 3-2 lead against the Cavaliers. The narrow lead that the Warriors had on the Cavs was unsafe, as everybody knew that LeBron James and his team could catch up at any moment they decide to. This is where the entire arena looked for their leader to step up and show the world exactly why he is the NBA's Most Valuable Player.

It was time for the best player of the world to carry his team over the hump, and put them in a definitive position to win it all the next game – and boy, did Steph deliver. His dazzling ball handling was on exhibition, putting Matthew Dellavedova (the player assigned to guard him) on skates. Confusing his opponent, and amazing his home fans, Steph casually steps back to the 3-point line and buries a 3-pointer right in the Cavs' face.

A cold-blooded dagger.

That 3-pointer officially sealed the door shut for any potential comeback by the Cavs, and the Warriors would go on to win the game with Curry finishing with 37 points and a series of highlight films for the ages.

He pounds his chest and points towards the sky once again. Once again his family was cheering for him at the top of their lungs, their faces beaming with pride and excitement.

Steph smiles, knowing full well he could not have won without them.

CHAPTER 6

IMPACT OF BASKETBALL

'Being a superstar means you've reached your potential, and I don't think I've reached my potential as a basketball player and as a leader yet.' – Stephen Curry

GREGG POPOVICH, the coach of the San Antonio Spurs, walked slowly to the swarm of reporters that awaited him. He hates doing these interviews, but understands that they come with the territory of being one of the greatest coaches in NBA history. He is usually known for his snide remarks or sarcastic comments, but this time he had a special mention for the Golden State Warriors. When asked about the 3-

point shot and how the Warriors use it to demolish their opponents, Popovich had nothing but disdain for it:

'I don't think it's basketball. I think it's kind of like a circus sort of thing. Why don't we have a 5-point shot? A 7-point shot? You know, where does it stop, that sort of thing. But that's just me, that's just old-school.'

One of the primary reasons Curry and the Warriors are so successful is because they utilize the 3-point shot better than any other team possibly in the history of the NBA. With Steph leading the charge, followed by Klay and other great teammates, they have literally stacked a group of players who are so versatile yet proficient in their 3-pointers, other teams would shiver at the thought of getting into a shootout with them – knowing full well they will lose. Also, Steve Kerr's coaching system of letting them run freely gives them the perfect pace and opportunity to fully maximize their 3-point capabilities. There may have been other good 3-point shooting teams in the history of the league before, but none of the calibre of the Warriors where the players and coaching staff are in perfect unison with one another. This kind of team really only comes around once in a lifetime.

As a result, many teams have decided to shrink their squad and opt for a fast-paced style of play, to match the Warriors' style of play. Some coaches, like Popovich, absolutely despise using the 3-pointer as their primary weapon, while other coaches are more open to the idea of having free-reign on the court.

Whatever the case may be, there will be no other team who shoots it better than Golden State, and this fact is further emphasized by having the best 3-point shooter on the entire planet in Stephen Curry.

Steph's antics at the 3-point line have not only earned him the nickname of a Splash Brother – he literally changed the landscape of how the game is played. Only when Steph came along and destroyed other teams with his supreme marksmanship did other teams realize just how powerful the 3-pointer really is.

Once the Warriors' staff realized the potential they had in Steph's ability, their offense became primarily centered around the 3-pointer, and under this system, Steph has become an absolute terror on the 3-point line. His quick release, and shooting form are pure perfection – even leaving other 3-point maestros' legacies such as Reggie Miller and Ray Allen in the dust.

Never before has a player with such supreme accuracy from downtown been given a supporting team and cast that fully empowers his 3-point abilities. Because of this, Curry and the Warriors have opened up an entirely new way of playing the game, and their dominance is still sending echoes throughout the league today – leaving other teams and other players wondering exactly how they can do the same.

With their current team record about to eclipse the best team record of all time set by Michael Jordan's Bulls back in the 90s, Steph and his Warriors have definitely made a dent in basketball's history, and left an impact that will be noticed for years to come.

CHAPTER 7

THE FUTURE

'I really cherish everything that basketball brings; and I think, for me, it's been a great ride and I'm not done yet'
– Stephen Curry

The Past

The Staples Center crowd waited in anticipation. One by one, Laker players run onto the court from inside the tunnels in their warm up jerseys. The excitement starts to build as the crowd stands and gives an ovation for Kobe's return. After facing a season ending injury against the Warriors in the previous season, Laker fans have waited eagerly for the Black Mamba to start spewing its venom once again. People from all ages, both young and old, have gathered to watch what could possibly be the legend's last season – just to catch one more glimpse of Kobe Bryant's magic on the court.

Finally, the announcer sounds *'At Guard, 6'6 out of Lower Merion High School. Number 24 - KOBEEEEEE BRYANNTTTTTT!'* The Staples Center erupts in excitement – The Black Mamba is back.

For the past 10 years or so, the NBA had been predominantly Kobe Bryant's league. Just like the great Michael Jordan who came before him, he brought in crowds that loved watching his signature brand of basketball and him exerting his dominance on other teams with his picturesque fade away.

Kobe's peak came in 2010, winning game 7 of the NBA Finals against the Boston Celtics and earning him his 5th Championship. The Celtics had defeated the Lakers back in 2008, and 2010 was Kobe's revenge – defeating the Celtics in a nail-biting game, and defeating his demons once and for all.

It was the perfect crowning moment for a 5-Time Champion, and it signified that finally it was time for him to pass the torch on to the next era, and see which player would take the league by storm.

* * *

The Present

That next player was none other than LeBron James. Coming straight out of high school to join the NBA, he immediately turned the Cleveland Cavaliers franchise around and gave the fans something new to be excited about. He also turned the entire basketball world on its head as soon as he announced his departure from Cleveland to join the Miami Heat, forming the first prominent "Big 3" of our modern era, with Dwyane Wade and Chris Bosh.

Many other stars followed LeBron's route and proceeded to form their own Big 3 as well – a testament to the effect LeBron had on the league. After Kobe's final championship, it was an undisputed fact that LeBron James would take over the reins as the best player in the world. Having gone to 6 NBA Finals and winning 2 back-to-back championships, his legacy has already been firmly cemented and placed in the hearts of fans all over the world.

Even now, at the age of only 31, James was unanimously elected as vice president of the players' union at a meeting he did not even attend. For the most part, it is still his league, and he will be reigning over it as the "King" for a couple more years to come.

However, after losing to the Warriors in the 2015 NBA Finals, suddenly everyone's attention turned to a new potential torch bearer for the league. While LeBron still has props as the greatest player in the world right now, another player is quickly making the case for his ascension to the NBA throne – Stephen Curry.

* * *

The Future

The victory Steph and his Warriors had over LeBron James' Cavs was also symbolic of the shifting of power throughout the league. Many fans and analysts thought that the Cavs would win after going up 2-1 in the Finals with LeBron having stellar back-to-back 40+ Point games.

Steph quickly erased those thoughts as he defeated the Cavs in definitive fashion, winning an NBA Championship, and denying the King of his grand prize. Suddenly talks began to arise about who is going to take over the league once LeBron is gone.

LeBron's athleticism is slowly winding down as he ages, while Steph's skills only seem to be rising. With his Warriors having the best record in the entire NBA, the stars in Golden State seem to shine brighter while the stars in Cleveland are slowly dimming down.

Analysts are now debating as to who exactly would carry the torch once LeBron's era is over. There are many other players viable for candidacy namely, Kevin Durant, Anthony Davis, Russell Westbrook or even James Harden. But among all those stars, only one player has made a massive impact on the league and a championship to show for it – Stephen Curry.

With his premier ball handling abilities, deadly shooting touch, relentless work ethic and a stellar cast of teammates all ready to take him to the next level, he is simply unmatched by all the other players and stands alone as the leading candidate to carry the league for years to come.

Being a fan favorite helps his campaign as well, as he constantly has one of the top All-Star voting numbers year after year and a fan base that absolutely adores him. Fans of the game want to watch Steph play, and marvel at his skills for years to come.

Stephen Curry undoubtedly, is the future of the NBA.

CONCLUSION

FINAL WORDS

'Success comes after you conquer your biggest obstacles and hurdles' – Stephen Curry

GAME 6, 2015 NBA FINALS – The Cavs fans at the Quicken Loans Arena hang their heads down in shame as they watch the Warriors mere minutes away from stealing a Championship right in front of their eyes.

It had been a long 40 years, 40 years since the Larry O'Brien Trophy had set foot in the Bay Area, and finally Stephen Curry and his Warriors were about to end that dry spell once and for all. This was all too familiar to Steph, ending the dry spell of his college team in Davidson and now doing the same thing on the biggest stage of basketball.

There was only about a minute left in the 4th quarter, and out of nowhere, the Cavs hit 2 difficult 3-pointers cutting the Warrior lead to just 4. The Warriors had held the lead for most of the game, and now in the final few seconds before they were to be crowned champions, the Cavaliers refused to quit. They scored 6 straight points and the Cavs fans were screaming in delight, holding on to whatever hope they had left of extending their season.

All the Warriors had to do was hang on – hang on for just 30 more seconds before officially winning the NBA Championship. Curry could almost taste the fruits of victory waiting for him, now all he had to do was make sure the Cavs' last barrage of attacks were not going to succeed.

Twenty seconds left. The Cavs hoist up a 3-pointer in desperation to cut the Warrior lead further, but to no avail. LeBron James tries to shoot another 3, but it simply bounces off the rim. The Cavs' efforts to catch up with 3s were in vain. Only the Warriors were able to score 3-pointers with such effortless skill and precision. Now with only 10 seconds left and a lead too far to catch up from, LeBron James congratulated Steph, pointed over to the Warrior bench and walked out of the court in pure disappointment.

Game Over. The Golden State Warriors were now NBA Champions.

The long, arduous and painful journey Stephen Curry had to go through had finally reached its peak – he was now an NBA Champion. No higher honor could be bestowed upon a team, and his MVP trophy was no higher honor that could be bestowed upon a player. For once, the doubters and critics that followed Steph throughout his entire career fell silent. There was simply nothing else to pick on.

Here was a man who was plagued with injury, whom the world had not even looked at, whose dreams were cast aside and yet, was able to come out on top, triumphant and victorious – his name forever etched in the highest honors of basketball. Now that the critics and doubters were quiet, Steph could enjoy his victory in absolute peace.

With all that has happened in Steph's life, the ups and downs, the injuries and the doubters, this may seem like a good end to his career. Wardell Stephen Curry is only 27 as this book is being written, and this is only the beginning of what's more to come in his already storied career. Who knows what else this NBA superstar has in store for us?

The Warriors are on track to make NBA history with the best team record of all time, eclipsing Michael Jordan's Chicago Bulls. Stephen Curry is still number 1 in MVP voting, and is probably due to achieve his 2nd consecutive MVP trophy. The Warriors look even better and sharper than they did last season – shocking everyone who thought that they got lucky by not facing the *actual* best teams in the Western Conference in the Spurs and Thunder. The Warriors shut them up for good this time, showing that *they* were the team to beat, and not the other way around. *They* are the best team in the league right now, and they have the best player in the world in Stephen Curry.

The future definitely looks bright for Stephen Curry and his Warriors.

From a simple kid with a love for the game of basketball, he was able to make his dreams become a reality with lots of hard work, discipline and commitment.

The journey wasn't easy. But despite everything that he's been through, it was definitely worth it.

Acknowledgments

Photo credits go to Keith Allison.
https://www.flickr.com/photos/keithallison/

Thanks for reading! Please add a short review on Amazon, and let me know what you thought!

JOHN EMERSON

Made in the USA
Middletown, DE
10 December 2016